A GIFT FOR:

FROM:

Hallmark

Copyright © 2015 Hallmark Licensing, LLC

Published by Hallmark Gift Books,
a division of Hallmark Cards, Inc.,
Kansas City, MO 64141
Visit us on the Web at Hallmark.com.

Editorial Director: Carrie Bolin
Editor: Emily Osborn
Art Director: Chris Opheim
Designer: Scott Swanson
Production Designer: Dan Horton
Contributing Writers: Chris Brethwaite,
Kevin Dilmore, Matt Gowen, Bill Gray,
Suzanne Heins, Debbie Lorenzi, and Molly Wigand

ISBN: 978-1-59530-723-1
BOK2187

Printed and bound in China
APR15

TWEET TALKIN'

ENCOURAGEMENT & INSPIRATION IN 140 CHARACTERS OR LESS

#06BeADreamer
#22BeMotivated
#38BeSuccessful
#52BeDaring

#66BeLogical
#80BeFlexible
#96BePositive
#112BeYou

AMER#BEADREAM

DON'T WALK THE
PATH TOWARD YOUR
DREAMS...RUN 'EM
DOWN AND TACKLE 'EM!
#GoU

It's impossible to follow your dreams and hang your head at the same time.

Your dreams are just out of your reach to encourage you to grow.

HAVING YOUR HEAD IN THE CLOUDS CAN HELP KEEP YOU ON YOUR TOES.

#Stretched2TheMax

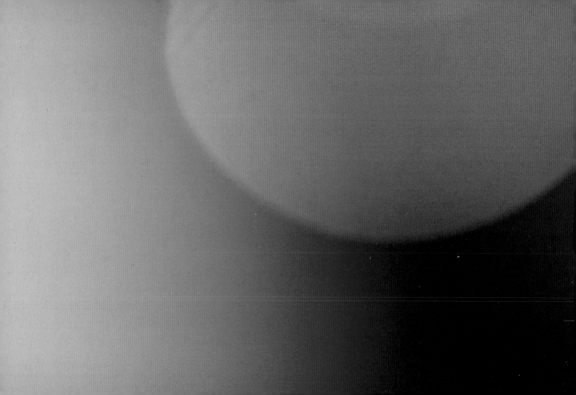

*Follow the flutter
of hope in your
heart...and
discover where
it leads.*

IF YOU CAN DREAM IT, YOU CAN DO IT. BUT FIRST YOU NEED TO WAKE UP AND GET OUT OF BED.

Dreams are the mind's caffeine. #EspressoAnyone

Curiosity may kill cats—but it can make imagination come alive.

THE PAST ISN'T A GREAT PLACE TO LIVE. BUT IT IS A GREAT PLACE TO VISIT.

#MoveAlong

ED#BEMOTIVATE

YOU CAN'T BUILD A BETTER TOMORROW WITHOUT HAMMERING A FEW NAILS TODAY.

#HammerTime

Nobody ever moved ahead by standing still. #StatingThe Obvious

If the grass is greener on the other side, move! #OrWaterYourYard

THEY WANT IT DONE
YOUR WAY OR THEY
WOULDN'T HAVE
ASKED YOU TO DO IT.
#JustLikeFrank

When you don't think you can do something, tell someone who will disagree.

YOU CAN SEE THE PATH SO MUCH CLEARER WHEN YOU LET NOTHING STAND IN YOUR WAY.

#BigYellowBulldozer

What doesn't kill you better run really fast when you're stronger.

Keep your head up because, for one thing, you have a really cute head.

NOTHING MAKES A PERSON MORE PRODUCTIVE THAN THE LAST MINUTE.

L#BESUCCESSFU

THERE'S NO SHORTCUT TO SUCCESS...JUST LIKE EATING COOKIES WON'T MAKE YOU SKINNY.

Hope floats, but success soars. #EnjoyTheView

Turns out the real secret to success is extra sleep. How cool is that? Very. #PowerNap

YOU MAY NOT GET
WHAT YOU WISH FOR,
BUT YOU ALWAYS GET
WHAT YOU WORK FOR.

Just because you have seeds of doubt doesn't mean you have to plant them.

DRESS FOR SUCCESS.
AT LEAST THAT
WAY IF YOU FAIL,
YOU'LL LOOK GOOD.
#FreeFashionAdvice

Remember, the only limits you have are on your credit cards.

Success is 10% inspiration, 95% perspiration, and 5% math.

EDARING#BEDAR

52

LIFE IS THE FABRIC.
WHAT WE MAKE OUT
OF IT IS UP TO US.
#BeCrafty

When you give your all, there is nothing to weigh you down. #LightAsAFeather

On the road of life, think of problems as traffic circles, not stop signs.

A DIAMOND IS JUST A LUMP OF COAL THAT DID WELL UNDER PRESSURE.

Make your own luck. It's not like somebody owns the patent on it.

YOU CAN'T RAISE THE BAR BY SITTING ON YOUR BUTT. #GetOffTheMat #WontRaiseItself

Climb every mountain. Repeat as needed.

If your life were a movie, this is the part where the lead actor would say, "Let's do this."

#IllBeBack

OGICAL#BELOGIC

EVERYTHING THAT HAPPENS TEACHES YOU HOW TO DEAL WITH EVERYTHING THAT HAPPENS.

Two heads are better than one. Plus, you get to drive in the carpool lane.

Never look back. That's not where you're headed.

IF YOU'RE JUST GOING THROUGH THE MOTIONS, MAYBE THEY'RE THE WRONG MOTIONS.

It pays to be greedy with criticism and generous with praise.

BEATING YOUR HEAD AGAINST THE WALL GETS YOU NOWHERE, EXCEPT MAYBE THE ER. #BeenThere

Never say "die"– unless it's a winning word on a quiz show. #GooniesLogic

Nobody knows the secret to life. What part of "secret" did you not get?

IBLE#BEFLEXIB

80

IF YOU CAN'T PERFORM MIRACLES, HARD WORK IS A GOOD SUBSTITUTE.

If life hands you lemons, Google "whiskey sour recipes." #cheers

Sometimes it takes being a big person to take only baby steps. #TheTortoiseWins

SLACK DOESN'T COST A THING, SO CUT YOURSELF AS MUCH AS YOU WANT.

Sometimes we make ourselves whole by giving ourselves a break.

REGARDLESS OF WHAT YOU HAMMER AWAY AT, YOU'RE BOUND TO HIT YOUR THUMB A TIME OR TWO.

50% of people make mistakes. The other 50% are liars. #WeAreHuman

Crap makes flowers stronger. Learn from flowers.

IF THE SNAG YOU JUST HIT IS YOUR BIGGEST PROBLEM OF THE DAY, YOU'RE DOING PRETTY DARN WELL. #Perspective

TIVE#BEPOSITI

E#BEPOSITIVE#

WHEN THE ROAD OF LIFE GETS TOO BUMPY, DRINK WITH A STRAW.

Don't look back . . . unless UR backing UR car up. #4ward

It takes two hands to push someone down, but only one to pull them up.

THE SUN WILL RISE
TOMORROW. IF IT
DOESN'T, WE'RE
ALL SCREWED.
#BrightSide

Nobody can do everything. But everyone can do something.
#YouCanToo

YOU CAN LICK
ANYTHING IF YOU
TRY. ASK ANY DOG.
#LifeIsDelicious

Being nice is, um, nice. Man, there must be a nicer word for it. #NicerThanNice

Life is as good as you decide it is.
#ChooseGreatness

KEEP A SMILE ON YOUR FACE TODAY! DON'T LET IT RUN OFF TO SOMEWHERE WEIRD, LIKE YOUR ARM.

#BEYOU#BEYOU#B

THE DIFFERENCE
BETWEEN YOU AND A
HOT PAN OF BROWNIES
IS THAT NO ONE HAS
TO WAIT 10 MINUTES
FOR YOU TO BE COOL.

Every tree in the forest is different, but each one reaches for the light.
#CommonPurpose

It's not how rich you are. It's how rich your heart is.

WHEN YOU FEED THE SOUL, ALWAYS GO FOR SECONDS.

#NoLeftovers

Thinking you can do something is proof you're either confident or delusional. #Sigmund

IT IS BETTER TO
FAIL IN ORIGINALITY
THAN TO SUCCEED
IN IMITATION.
#HermanMelville
#JustBeYou

Nobody ever got lost following their heart's desire. #DreamOn

Here's the thing: There's a reason there's only one you. Figure it out.